History of Britain

Roman Britain

55BC to AD 406

Brenda Williams

HAMLYN

HISTORY OF BRITAIN — ROMAN BRITAIN
was produced for Hamlyn Children's Books
by Lionheart Books, London.

Editor: Lionel Bender
Designer: Ben White
Picture Researcher: Jennie Karrach
Media Conversion and Typesetting:
   Peter MacDonald

Educational Consultant: Jane Shuter
Editorial Advisors: Andrew Farrow, Paul Shuter

Production Controller: Linda Spillane
Managing Editor: David Riley

First Published in Great Britain in 1994
by Hamlyn Children's Books,
an imprint of Reed Children's Books Limited,
Michelin House, 81 Fulham Road, London SW3 6RB,
and Auckland, Melbourne, Singapore and Toronto.

Copyright © 1994 Reed International Books Limited.

ISBN 0 600 58085 7 (HB)
ISBN 0 600 58086 5 (PB)

British Library Cataloguing-in-Publication Data.
A catalogue record for this book is available
from the British Library.

Acknowledgements
Picture credits Page 7: Peter Reynolds/Mick Sharp Photos. p8/9: By
Courtesy of the Trustees of the British Museum. p9: from Llyn Cerrig
Bach, Anglesey, Courtesy of the National Museum of
Wales. p10: By Courtesy of the Trustees of the British Museum. p11:
Aerofilms Limited. p13: Michael Holford. p15: By Courtesy of the
Trustees of the British Museum. p15 (left): Dorset Natural History and
Archaelogical Society. p16,17: Museum of London. p18: Colchester
Museums. p19: The Mansell Collection. p21: Scala, Italy – Museum
delle Terme. p22: By Courtesy of the Trustees of the British Museum.
p25: Aerofilms Limited. p26: Mick Sharp. p28: Verulamium Museum,
Courtesy of City and District Council of St Albans. p30: Mick Sharp.
p31: Lesley and Roy Adkins Picture Library. p32: © The National Trust
Photographic Library. p34: Michael Holford. p36: Ashmoleum Museum,
Oxford. p38: St Albans Museum. p40: Museum of London. p41: By
Courtesy of the Trustees of the British Museum. p42: Aerofilms Limited.
p43 (top): The Bridgeman Art Library/Bibliothèque Municipale, Rouen.
p43 (bottom): By Courtesy of the Trustees of the British Museum.
Cover: Verulamium Museum, Courtesy of City and District Council of St
Albans; Jean Williamson/Mick Sharp (ruins of Roman theatre); Museum
of London (sword and scabbard).
Artwork credits Stefan Chabluk: maps p4, 45. Mark Bergin: 12/13,
18/19 James Field: 2, 5, 8/9, 10/11, 16/17, 20/21, 28/29, 42/43, 46.
Bill Donohoe: 24/25, 30/31, 36/37. John James: 1, 4, 6/7, 14/15,
22/23, 26/27, 32/33, 34/35, 38/39, 40/41. Malcolm Smythe: page 45.
Hayward Art: page 44 and small maps. Cover: Design by Peter Bennett,
Artwork by Stephen Conlin.

CONTENTS

The Roman Period

Everyday objects made in Roman Britain are sometimes found in the ground. Long-lost buildings can be traced in photos taken from the air. Ruins may be uncovered by digging during rebuilding work.

The illustrations in this book are based on historical evidence. They have been painted by artists who have used descriptions from Roman times and archaeological evidence to help them decide how things looked.

ROMAN BRITAIN	SAXONS AND VIKINGS	MEDIEVAL BRITAIN	THE TUDORS	THE STUARTS	THE GEORGIANS	VICTORIAN BRITAIN	MODERN BRITAIN
55BC to AD406	406 to 1066	1066 to 1485	1485 to 1603	1603 to 1714	1714 to 1837	1837 to 1901	1901 to the 1990s

ABOUT THIS BOOK

This book considers Roman Britain chronologically, meaning that events are described in the order in which they happened, from 55 BC to AD 406. However, most of the double-page articles deal with aspects of everyday life, such as soldiering, trade, houses and food. These things did not change greatly during the time the Romans ruled Britain. Unfamiliar words are explained in the glossary on page 46.

All dates are based on the birth of Jesus Christ as a starting point. Events before this are dated backwards from it. These dates are given the letters BC, which are short for Before Christ. So 200 BC is earlier than 100 BC. Events after the birth of Christ are dated with the letters AD, from the Latin words *anno domini*, meaning 'in the year of the Lord'. Towards the end of the book, where events described happened in more recent times, all the dates are AD unless it says otherwise.

About the map

This shows the location of places mentioned in the text. The names in brackets are those used by the Romans. They are in Latin. Some of the places on the map are large towns, others smaller towns or the sites of battles or famous ruins and places of interest.

MAP OF BRITAIN

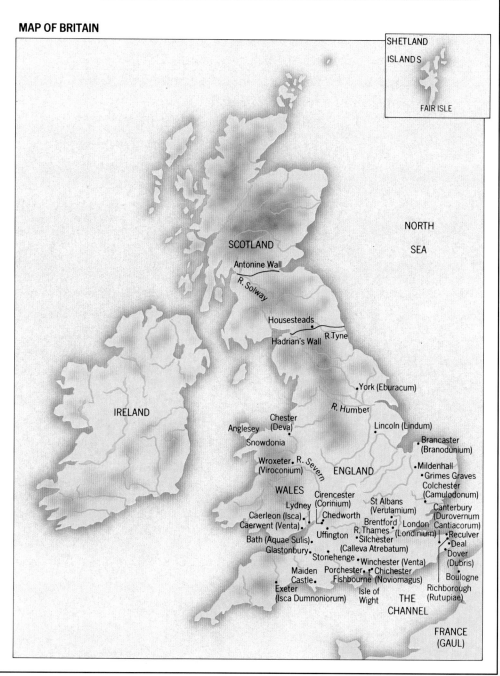

INTRODUCTION

The Romans ruled much of the British Isles for almost 400 years, from AD 43 until the early 400s. Before the Romans, other peoples, known as Celts, had come to Britain from mainland Europe. They lived in large groups, called tribes, each of which had its own territory or kingdom.

The Romans had a huge empire, which spread from Rome across Italy, through Europe and to parts of Africa and Asia. In all the countries they took over, they introduced their own customs and their language, Latin.

The Romans first invaded Britain in 55 BC but soon left. They returned in AD 43. This time they took over all of England and Wales, but they did not have enough soldiers to make Scotland or Ireland part of their empire.

The Romans brought peace to Britain. They built towns and roads. Many British people, especially in the south, copied the Roman way of life and even followed the Roman religions. They became 'Romanized'. But as the Roman empire grew bigger, it became harder to govern. People in the countries ruled from Rome became more troublesome. Rome had to take away soldiers from the edges of the empire to defend lands closer to Italy. This left countries such as Britain badly defended and open to invasion by other peoples.

In the AD 400s, Rome lost control of both Gaul (now France) and Britain. Other peoples from Europe – Angles, Saxons and Jutes – invaded, and Roman Britain came to an end.

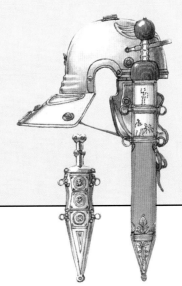

BEFORE THE ROMANS

The first people of Britain lived among its forests and hills. They hunted, fished and gathered wild plants. About 4000 BC, people with stone axes began clearing the forests to grow crops and graze cattle. By 2500 BC, Britons used copper and bronze tools. They turned the forests into farms, fields, woods and pasture.

Stone-using farmers made their tools with flint from mines like Grimes Graves in Norfolk. They buried their dead in huge tombs of earth or rocks. The bronze-users dug round burial mounds called barrows. They also built Stonehenge and other stone circles.

Iron tools were made by people called Celts, whose homeland was in central Europe. By about 500 BC, the Celts had moved westward and into Britain. They lived in tribes, or large groups, which often fought each other for the lands they settled.

△ **Bronze wheel hub and horse bits.** The Celts used bronze to decorate swords, shields, harnesses and horse-trappings.

▽ **In a Celtic village**
● homes were mostly round, with thatched roofs
● walls were made of stone, or wattle (woven branches) and daub (clay or mud cement)
● a wooden fence was put up between the homes and land beyond
● ox-wagons carried supplies from the fields
● farm animals were kept in enclosures for safety
● craftsmen made tools, horseshoes and pots
● villagers made huts, threshed corn, ground grain and brewed beer.

The Celts were good fighters and farmers, and loved feasting. Their skilled blacksmiths made iron weapons as well as farm tools. They also made beautifully decorated armour, buckles and brooches. Celtic farmers made the first fields in Britain that were sowed in turn from year to year, instead of clearing new land when the old soil wore out.

With iron tools, farmers could work heavier soils and grow better crops. They stored wheat and barley in pits for winter use. They also grew turnips, beans, cabbages and parsnips. They kept sheep, goats, pigs and cattle to give meat, milk, wool and leather.

The Celts lived in round huts, on single farms or in village groups. They built an earth bank and ditch or fence around their homes, as at Butser Ancient Farm in Hampshire. The lake village at Glastonbury in Somerset was built on marshy islands. In Scotland, some homes were built on islands in lochs.

◁ **At Butser Ancient Farm**, there are modern copies of the Celtic houses and fences that stood there more than 2,000 years ago.

CELTIC EVERYDAY LIFE

Most Celts in Britain worked on their farms. When day ended, they enjoyed feasting, drinking, singing and story-telling. These proud people admired the brave and strong. They were loyal to their tribe and its chief. Religion was important to everyone.

People worked in the village as well as in the fields. They built and mended huts and wagons. They made iron tools or pottery or carved wood. Children kept watch on grazing cattle or sheep, or helped their parents. They ground grain for flour, baked bread and wove brightly patterned cloth for the tunics and cloaks everyone wore. The Celts liked to look attractive. Few of them were dirty or ragged. When they washed they used soap – unlike the Romans.

Meals were cooked over a fire inside the home. Smoke escaped through a hole in the roof. Meat from the farm or the hunt was baked, roasted on a spit, or stewed in a pot. People ate their food from wooden bowls, sitting on the floor.

△ **Gold torcs**, or neck rings, were worn by important people. Some warriors fought wearing nothing else.

▷ **In a family hut**, stew cooks in a pot over the fire, while a daughter weaves cloth on her loom. A hunting dog keeps guard. The Celts were proud of their looks, especially their long fair hair. They used bronze mirrors like the one shown below.

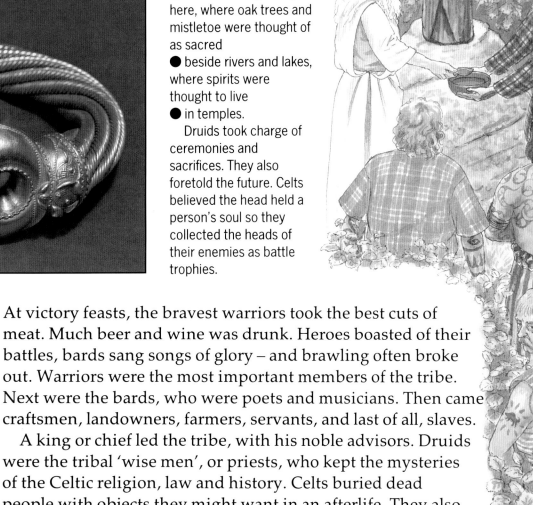

▷ **Celts worshipped as many as 400 gods**
● in woodland groves, as here, where oak trees and mistletoe were thought of as sacred
● beside rivers and lakes, where spirits were thought to live
● in temples.
Druids took charge of ceremonies and sacrifices. They also foretold the future. Celts believed the head held a person's soul so they collected the heads of their enemies as battle trophies.

At victory feasts, the bravest warriors took the best cuts of meat. Much beer and wine was drunk. Heroes boasted of their battles, bards sang songs of glory – and brawling often broke out. Warriors were the most important members of the tribe. Next were the bards, who were poets and musicians. Then came craftsmen, landowners, farmers, servants, and last of all, slaves.

A king or chief led the tribe, with his noble advisors. Druids were the tribal 'wise men', or priests, who kept the mysteries of the Celtic religion, law and history. Celts buried dead people with objects they might want in an afterlife. They also killed animals and humans, to offer as sacrifices to their gods. Each year they held four great festivals. One of these – the Feast of Samhain – is remembered in our Hallowe'en.

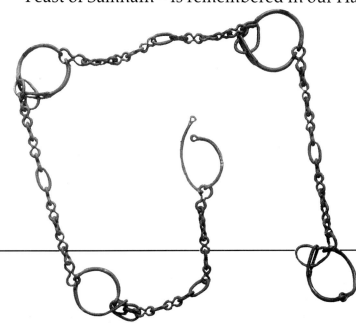

◁ **Iron slave-gang chain** found in the Druid stronghold of Anglesey, Wales. The Celts in Britain sold their slaves, shown right, to peoples across the Channel. This chain was found among a hoard of metal objects in a peat bog. Celts may have thrown them into the bog as offerings to the gods.

A Military Hill-fort

Rival tribes were often at war. They built hill-top forts which were good lookout posts and places to defend. Some forts were defended farms. Others became larger settlements, more like villages or towns. The largest – among them Maiden Castle in Dorset – were tribal centres, home of the local chief.

Hill-fort builders dug a ditch round the hill and piled the earth into a bank on one side. Along the top they put a fence of sharp stakes, or a stone wall. In the north and in Wales, they used wood and stone to strengthen the bank. Some hill-forts had three or four rings of banks and ditches. Maiden Castle also had maze-like gateways and barriers.

Hill-forts were built all over Britain. England and Wales alone had more than 1,400. Many fort sites can still be seen.

Celtic weapons and armour included
● slings and stones
● iron-tipped spears and long slashing swords
● metal helmets
● shields of wood or leather, faced with bronze and decorated in swirling patterns.

Warriors often fought without armour. They painted their bodies with dye and limed their hair into thick, stiff 'manes'.

◁ **A highly decorated Celtic shield** fished from the River Thames at Battersea, London.

△ **Celtic charioteers** drove two-wheeled vehicles behind pairs of horses. Their fast driving and manoeuvring were admired by the invading Romans, who had never faced war chariots before.

▷ **Celtic men wore trousers and tunics and women loose dresses.** Everyone wore a cloak, and shoes made of leather or linen. Men grew long moustaches but not beards.

◁ **The White Horse** in the chalk hillside at Uffington, Berkshire, is 110 metres long. It may have been cut by the Atrebates – a Celtic tribe – to show that they ruled the area.

▽ **The hill-fort at Maiden Castle, Dorset**, was probably the tribal home of the Durotriges. The fort covers an area the size of 25 football pitches. Within it, local markets were held.

Celtic families were always ready for danger. When under attack, they fled to the local hill-fort with all the belongings they could take – even sheep and cattle.

Celts gloried in battle. Their armies put on a great show – shouting terrible war cries, trumpeting horns, clashing swords on shields. Warrior Celts looked terrifying too, with streaming hair and painted bodies. They wanted enemies to flee in fear. Tribal arguments might be settled by single combat. If there was a battle, every fighter wanted glory – and enemy heads to take home.

Celtic fighters were skilled horsemen, especially the charioteers. Britons used war chariots long after the Celts across the Channel had given them up for mounted horsemen only. In 54 BC, the British chief Cassivellaunus had 4,000 chariots at his command.

As they raced a chariot into battle, the driver and warrior on board hurled spears or slingshots. The warrior then jumped down to fight on foot with the infantry. The driver led the chariot away and waited to rescue his passenger or take him to another part of the battlefield.

CAESAR'S ARMY INVADES

"Along the cliffs, I saw the enemy troops, heavily armed", wrote Julius Caesar. Britain became part of the Roman world in 55 BC, when Julius Caesar landed his army on its shores. Caesar's books about his wars tell us most of what we know about Britain in these times. His army soon left – but the Romans were one day to return.

The Britons knew Caesar was coming. He sent word of his invasion plans to as many tribes as possible, hoping they would surrender. Meanwhile, he gathered his forces in Gaul.

One autumn morning, two Roman legions (about 10,000 soldiers) in 80 ships sailed past Dover. Thousands of warriors were waiting on the cliffs. The ships stopped along the coast near Deal. Chasing them on land came the Celts.

Caesar's soldiers had to wade ashore through deep water in armour. Facing them were the Celts in full cry, hurling spears. The Romans held back. Then the standard-bearer of the Tenth Legion leapt into the sea and shouted for the rest of the men to follow. Cheering, they did.

▷ **Roman soldiers and British warriors about to do battle** on the beaches near Deal in Kent in 55 BC.

Caesar's raid in 54 BC. He took with him 30,000 men. His fleet sailed from Boulogne in Gaul (France) at sunset and landed in Kent at dawn. The Roman soldiers moved swiftly inland, crossing the River Thames possibly at Brentford.

▷ **The Roman world after Caesar's landings in Britain.** Until 55 BC, Britain was a mystery to most Romans. But Britons had helped the Gauls in France fight Caesar. Rebel Gauls also found refuge in Britain. To end such alliances, Caesar planned the invasion. Rome also wanted Britain's grain, cattle and metals.

BRITANNIA (Britain)

MACEDONIA (Greece)

GAUL (France)

HISPANIA (Spain)

ITALIA (Italy)

JUDAEA (Israel, Lebanon)

AFRICA NOVA (Tunisia)

CYRENAICA (Libya)

AEGYPTUS (Egypt)

◁ **Julius Caesar**
- was born in 100 BC
- was a powerful politician by 59 BC
- in 58 BC became a general and conquered Gaul
- invaded Britain in 55 BC and again in 54 BC
- in 49 BC took control of the Roman government
- met Queen Cleopatra of Egypt in 48 BC
- won his last battle, in Spain, in 45 BC
- was murdered in 44 BC by nobles who feared he might become king.

Once ashore, a bloody battle took place, but the legions' steady attack won the day. The Celts asked for peace. But then storms damaged Caesar's ships and stopped more troops from reaching him. The Celts realized his army was stranded and attacked again. Caesar won again, but knew he would soon be defeated, and so sailed for Gaul the same day.

The next spring Caesar came back with over 800 ships, 5 legions and 2,000 cavalry. This time the Britons tried fighting together under one leader, Cassivellaunus.

The fighting ended when tribal enemies of Cassivellaunus, the Trinovantes, made peace. Caesar took British hostages and tribute (a yearly tax), then sailed away. Nearly 100 years were to pass before the Romans returned.

◁ **Roman warships** had sails, oars and a prow at the front for ramming enemy ships. Each ship carried hundreds of troops.

13

THE CONQUEST OF CLAUDIUS

"Why, when you have all this, do you envy us our poor huts?", asked the British chief Caratacus when he saw the city of Rome. Between the Roman invasions of 55 BC and AD 43, Britain changed as tribes in the south-east gained more lands and power.

Everyday life in much of Britain went on as before. But in the south-east, large settlements became the strongholds of local chiefs and kings. Among them were places later called St Albans, Canterbury and Colchester. The Trinovantes of Essex were still Rome's allies. They fought their old enemies, the Catuvellauni of Hertfordshire, for Colchester, but lost. The victors' leader, Cunobelinus, became chief of both tribes.

▽ **Claudius leads his troops into Colchester.** After Claudius's triumph, one legion, the 20th, stayed in Colchester. The 9th and 14th legions moved into the north and west Midlands. The 2nd, led by the future emperor Vespasian, marched south-west to capture the Isle of Wight and hill-forts, including Maiden Castle.

△ **After landing in Kent** the Romans massed at Canterbury. They crossed the River Medway and then the Thames, to enter Colchester.

Later, Cunobelinus quarrelled with one of his sons, who fled to the emperor Caligula in Rome. Caligula got ready to invade Britain, but changed his mind. Then he was murdered, and his uncle Claudius became emperor. Soon after, Cunobelinus died and his son Caratacus seized lands from another of Rome's British allies. Claudius needed strong allies in Britain for trade to flourish, as well as a victory in battle to keep his throne. He ordered an army to set sail for Britain.

In the summer of AD 43, about 40,000 Roman soldiers sailed from Gaul and landed at Richborough, Kent. They fought hard to defeat Caratacus in a two-day battle at the River Medway, and then marched on to the River Thames. Caratacus fled to Wales, where he fought the Romans for another eight years.

Claudius himself came from Rome to lead his troops into Colchester. Eleven British kings surrendered to him. After 16 days, Claudius left Britain. His army remained.

▷ **A sculpture of the head of Claudius**, made about AD 41, the year he became emperor. Being lame, Claudius had led the quiet life of a scholar and was often treated as a fool. But for his victory in Britain, Rome's Senate (government) gave him the title *Britannicus*.

◁ **Signs of the fierce battle to take Maiden Castle** include this section of a skeleton, which still has the bolt from a Roman ballista (catapult) stuck in its backbone. The hill-fort defenders piled sling shot stones in dumps.

THE BRITONS REVOLT

The Romans soon took over southern England. Many tribal chiefs decided that to keep power they should side with the Romans. One such ally was Prasutagus of the Iceni in Norfolk. His queen, Boudicca, was described by a Roman as "very tall…her voice was harsh…a great mass of red hair fell to her hips".

Claudius made Colchester the capital of the new Roman province of Britannia. But a site on the Thames proved better for merchants. This site, London, grew as the centre for business and trade.

Caratacus was still in Wales and causing trouble. A few tribes joined him in a big battle against the Romans near the River Severn in AD 51. The Romans won easily, and Caratacus fled north to the Brigantes tribe. But their queen, Cartimandua, handed him over to the Romans, who were her allies. Caratacus was taken to Rome in chains.

The Britons in Wales still fought Roman rule. In AD 60, the governor of Britain, Suetonius Paulinus, attacked Anglesey. This was a Druid stronghold, from which the priests inspired the Britons in their fight against the Romans.

Paulinus described his enemies like this: "On the shore stood the enemy. Between the ranks dashed women in black, like the Furies, with their hair let down and streaming and brandishing flaming torches. Around the enemy host were Druids, uttering prayers and curses."

Paulinus and his men destroyed the Druid base. Then they heard that the Iceni of Norfolk were in revolt, led by their queen, Boudicca.

▷ **Sword blade and metal part of its scabbard (cover)** found in the Thames at Fulham. They belonged to a Roman officer who may have been killed when Boudicca's army swept through London, burning the settlement.

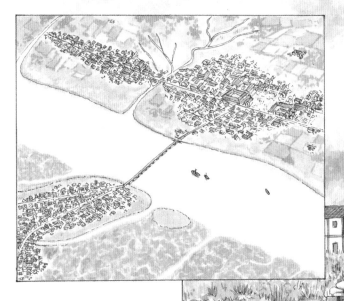

△ **Roman London about AD 50.** The Romans built a bridge across the Thames, and a busy port-town grew on the north bank of the river.

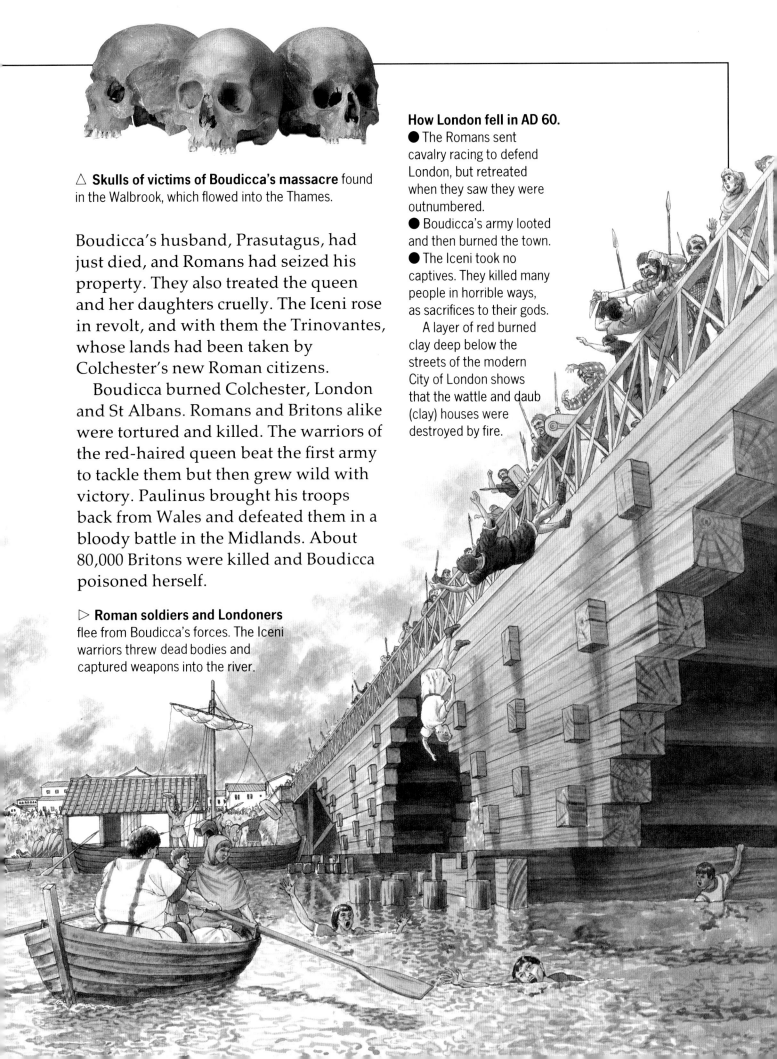

△ **Skulls of victims of Boudicca's massacre** found in the Walbrook, which flowed into the Thames.

Boudicca's husband, Prasutagus, had just died, and Romans had seized his property. They also treated the queen and her daughters cruelly. The Iceni rose in revolt, and with them the Trinovantes, whose lands had been taken by Colchester's new Roman citizens.

Boudicca burned Colchester, London and St Albans. Romans and Britons alike were tortured and killed. The warriors of the red-haired queen beat the first army to tackle them but then grew wild with victory. Paulinus brought his troops back from Wales and defeated them in a bloody battle in the Midlands. About 80,000 Britons were killed and Boudicca poisoned herself.

▷ **Roman soldiers and Londoners** flee from Boudicca's forces. The Iceni warriors threw dead bodies and captured weapons into the river.

How London fell in AD 60.
● The Romans sent cavalry racing to defend London, but retreated when they saw they were outnumbered.
● Boudicca's army looted and then burned the town.
● The Iceni took no captives. They killed many people in horrible ways, as sacrifices to their gods.

A layer of red burned clay deep below the streets of the modern City of London shows that the wattle and daub (clay) houses were destroyed by fire.

THE ROMANS TAKE CONTROL

After Boudicca's revolt, the Romans took a firmer hold on southern Britain. At first they punished the Britons, by burning villages and farms. Then they began to govern more justly to gain favour with more British chieftains. "They create grief and ruin and call it peace", grumbled Calgacus, a northern leader.

Southern Britain was peaceful. Now the Romans turned to the north and west, which were still free from Roman rule.

Wales was rich in minerals that included gold, silver and copper. There was also lead and tin, from which bronze could be made. Governor Frontinus, and Agricola after him, gained control of Wales in the AD 70s. Agricola was a Gaul from southern France and one of Rome's best generals. He led an army into the mountains of Snowdonia and crushed the last British resistance.

▷ **A Welsh frontier fort.** From about AD 74 the 2nd Augusta Legion was based at Caerleon in Wales, where remains of the fort can still be seen.

Early forts had a wooden fence and tents, but from about AD 100 many were rebuilt in stone A big fort measured roughly 600 metres long and 400 metres wide. Inside were stables, barracks, storerooms, hospital and cookhouse.

▷ **Tombstone** of Longinus, a cavalryman from Bulgaria, who died in Colchester. His carved tombstone shows a Roman horseman defeating a cowering enemy.

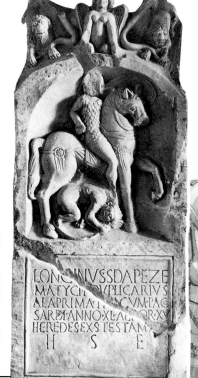

▽ **Plan of the fort at Caerleon** with barracks, storerooms and offices.

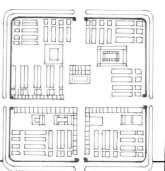

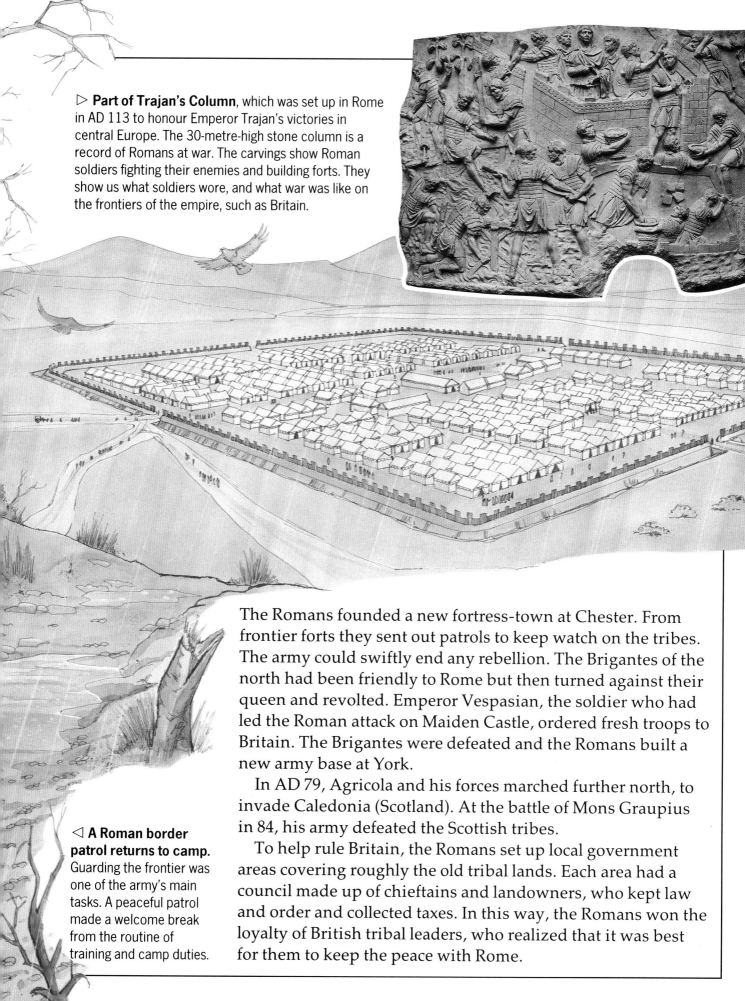

▷ **Part of Trajan's Column**, which was set up in Rome in AD 113 to honour Emperor Trajan's victories in central Europe. The 30-metre-high stone column is a record of Romans at war. The carvings show Roman soldiers fighting their enemies and building forts. They show us what soldiers wore, and what war was like on the frontiers of the empire, such as Britain.

◁ **A Roman border patrol returns to camp.** Guarding the frontier was one of the army's main tasks. A peaceful patrol made a welcome break from the routine of training and camp duties.

The Romans founded a new fortress-town at Chester. From frontier forts they sent out patrols to keep watch on the tribes. The army could swiftly end any rebellion. The Brigantes of the north had been friendly to Rome but then turned against their queen and revolted. Emperor Vespasian, the soldier who had led the Roman attack on Maiden Castle, ordered fresh troops to Britain. The Brigantes were defeated and the Romans built a new army base at York.

In AD 79, Agricola and his forces marched further north, to invade Caledonia (Scotland). At the battle of Mons Graupius in 84, his army defeated the Scottish tribes.

To help rule Britain, the Romans set up local government areas covering roughly the old tribal lands. Each area had a council made up of chieftains and landowners, who kept law and order and collected taxes. In this way, the Romans won the loyalty of British tribal leaders, who realized that it was best for them to keep the peace with Rome.

19

THE ROMAN ARMY

By AD 100 a Roman army had settled in Britain. Its task was to defend this northern frontier of Rome's empire and keep the peace. The Romans had paid, full-time, trained soldiers, unlike many of the peoples they fought. Roman discipline and organization triumphed in battle over Celtic dash and fury.

△ **A Roman soldier in north Britain** stands before the gates of his fort, ready to march. He wears armour to protect his body and shoulders. In his right hand he carries a javelin. His curved shield is made of wooden strips, covered in leather and with metal strengthening.

A legionary in Britain
● wore armour made of metal plates linked by leather straps beneath
● had a helmet with ear and cheek guards
● marched at roughly 7 kilometres an hour
● ate bread, porridge, bacon fat, soup, cheese and vegetables.

△ **A legionary's kit.**
A Roman soldier on the march often carried his helmet strapped to one shoulder. His kit hung from a pole he rested on his other shoulder. In leather bags tied to the pole were clothes, food dish, cooking pot, rations and digging tools.

The Roman army in Britain had three main fort-bases: at Chester, Caerleon and York. Other bases at Gloucester and Lincoln became towns in which retired soldiers lived. Soldiers were grouped into legions, each with 5,000 to 6,000 men (legionaries). There were three legions in Britain. Every legion had ten units called cohorts, each commanded by a centurion. A legion had 120 horsemen, who acted as scouts and messengers.

Foot-soldiers (infantry) won most Roman battles. At the battle of Mons Graupius in Scotland in AD 84, Agricola himself led the infantry. They charged uphill, stabbing and hacking their way through the enemy ranks. Meanwhile, the Roman cavalry (horsemen) drove off the British chariots. The Romans claimed 10,000 British dead, for the loss of only 400 Roman lives.

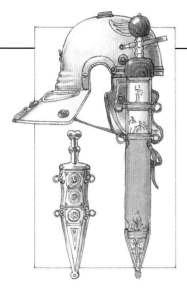

△ **A Roman soldier's helmet, and his sword and dagger** in their scabbards. His main weapons were a short sword and a long javelin. He threw his javelin at the enemy, then rushed forward to use his sword. He did not slash but stabbed with its point.

△ **Each legion had its own flags and standards**, like the one shown above. The first cohort guarded the gold aquila, or eagle. To be the standard-bearer was a great honour. For a legion to lose its aquila in battle was a terrible disgrace and a bad omen.

As they marched across Britain, the legions took their artillery with them. These were the huge wooden catapults and slingers used to attack hill-forts. Each night in enemy country the soldiers set up camp. They made trenches and earth banks around the camp to defend the neat rows of tents.

The Roman army in Britain used many 'auxiliary' troops. These soldiers came from all over the empire, including Spain, Greece, Turkey and Africa.

Soldiers often joined the Roman army as teenagers and served for 25 years. Out of their salary they had to pay for the bedding, food, boots and clothing that the army supplied. Each man paid money to a burial fund and for a yearly camp dinner. Training was hard. It included marching, use of weapons, swimming and tree-felling.

In a frontier province like Britain, an army general also had to be a politician and governor. He dealt with local problems as well as matters of empire.

◁ **Battle scenes on Trajan's Column** show Romans in fierce hand-to-hand fights. Legionaries advanced behind a wall of shields, trampling the enemy underfoot.

▽ **A certificate of citizenship**, given to a soldier on retirement. Legionaries were retired, with a pension, when they were too old or too badly injured to fight.

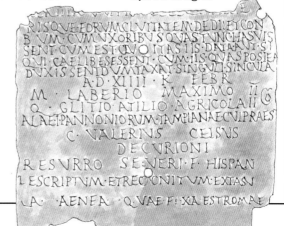

BRITAIN BECOMES ROMAN

The Romans did not stay in Scotland or invade Ireland. Their British province included only England and Wales. There, many Britons soon took up Roman ways and, in turn, the Romans grew used to Britain's customs and climate. With them they brought Roman fashions, building styles, law, religion and home life.

In the countryside, the invasion wars had damaged farms and villages. The Romans had destroyed many British hill-forts and turned others into their own army bases. Like all conquerors, the Roman rulers of Britain took large estates for themselves. Often the men, women and children who had lived on these lands were taken as slaves.

However, the Romans wanted British farming to recover quickly. Their army needed food and so did the growing numbers of people in the towns. British warriors were sent back to their farms to plough and plant the fields.

The Romans took over old British settlements and turned them into towns. One of the biggest and richest was Cirencester. But even a small town such as Caerwent in Wales had elegant houses, like those found in Rome itself.

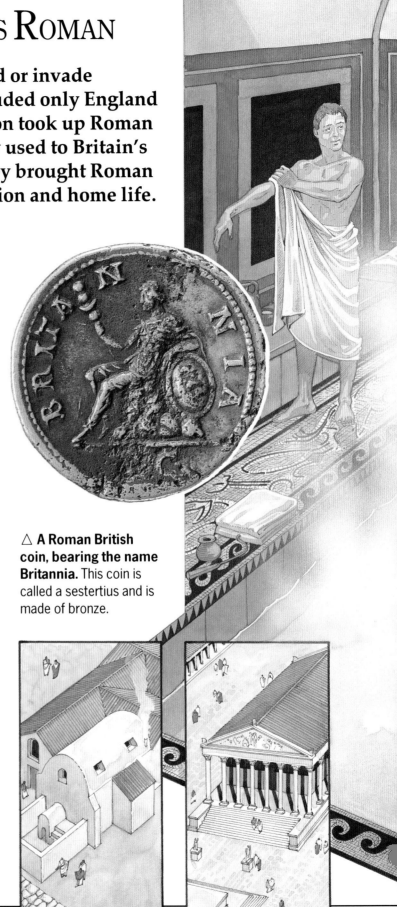

△ **A Roman British coin, bearing the name Britannia.** This coin is called a sestertius and is made of bronze.

▷ **Some ways in which the Romans made Britain more civilized:**
● in towns, they built plumbing systems to supply drinking water and for bath-houses, like that shown on the right
● they put up public buildings, like the temple at Colchester (far right)

● they built a system of good roads
● they introduced central heating
● in some towns, they built amphitheatres for entertainment
● they developed trade and industry
● they stopped tribal wars.

▽ **In the baths, people**
● used oil and scrapers called strigils, not soap, to clean themselves
● could spend the whole day relaxing and, if wealthy, were waited on by their servants
● played board games
● kept fit with exercises
● had a massage.
There was a small entrance fee to the baths.

◁ **Inside, the bath-house** was elegantly decorated with mosaic tiles. Heating in the rooms varied from warm (as here), hot and dry, steamy, to cool.

As Britain was 'Romanized', people in the towns took to wearing Roman-style clothes and furnished their homes in the Roman way. Whether they lived in towns or the countryside, Romans in Britain wanted the same comforts as in other parts of the empire. Traders brought fine pottery, beautiful silks and silverware from the Continent. Merchants travelled to Britain from all over Europe and beyond. Some of these foreign traders settled in British towns. Soon there were groups of newcomers, including Italians and Greeks, living in the larger British towns such as Bath, York and London.

One clear sign that Britain had become Romanized was the building of bath-houses in every town. The Celts were a clean people, but to the Romans a bath-house was not just a place to wash. They went there to relax, to talk business or politics, or simply gossip. The town of Bath, known to the Romans as Aquae Sulis, was a health resort. People visited the baths (which can still be seen) as they believed the waters from local hot springs could cure all kinds of diseases.

▷ **In the new Roman Britain** many people soon adopted Roman styles and fashions. The rich, and people who worked for the Romans, took to wearing a toga, which was a loose wrap-around piece of cloth. Men shaved and cut their hair rather short. Poorer people, however, continued to wear the Celtic style of clothes.

THE EDGE OF THE EMPIRE

In AD 122, Emperor Hadrian ordered a wall to be built across northern England to mark the frontier of Roman rule. Hadrian's Wall, much of which can still be seen, is the most astounding achievement of the Romans in Britain.

Hadrian's Wall took eight years to build. The Romans wanted to control movement and trade between England and Scotland, so the wall was to be a frontier checkpoint that soldiers could defend if necessary. The wall followed a line from the River Tyne in the east to the River Solway in the west.

Soldiers did the building using local materials – stone in the east and mostly turf in the west. Along the wall were fortified gateways, now called milecastles, with living quarters for soldiers. Between each pair of milecastles were two turrets, used as watchtowers.

△ **A milecastle on Hadrian's Wall**, with its gateway and barracks. The wall was built to control movement, not stop it. Traders, travellers and farmers passed through the gates – but probably had to pay a toll either in money or goods. The big milecastles housed up to 100 troops.

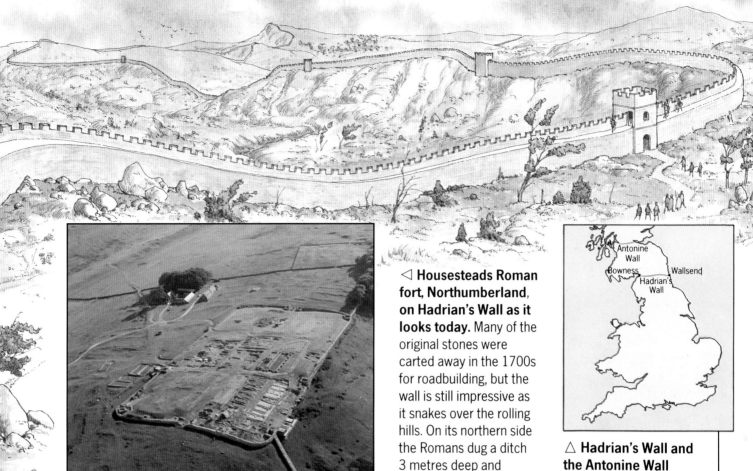

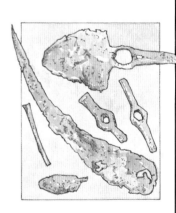

◁ **Housesteads Roman fort, Northumberland, on Hadrian's Wall as it looks today.** Many of the original stones were carted away in the 1700s for roadbuilding, but the wall is still impressive as it snakes over the rolling hills. On its northern side the Romans dug a ditch 3 metres deep and 9 metres wide. On the southern side was a straight flat-bottomed ditch. This may have been a boundary marker.

△ **Hadrian's Wall and the Antonine Wall** further north. Hadrian's Wall stretches east-west 118 kilometres, from the present-day towns of Bowness to Wallsend.

The soldiers guarding the wall had little fighting to do. Their main tasks were to check who went north or south, keep the peace, and repair the wall. Until about AD 120, few Britons were Roman citizens, so the first troops on the wall were mostly auxiliaries. The legionaries who built Hadrian's Wall were trained for battle and were too important to patrol it.

The weather in the north could be cold and wet. In winter, the forts were snow-bound and the barrack rooms were cold. Soldiers off duty probably crowded into any hut with a fire. Bath-houses were probably the cosiest places. Outside, the troops were glad of their woollen cloaks, worn over leather tunics and woollen trousers.

Soldiers kept their own farm animals. They ate well – meat from cows, sheep, goats, pigs and chickens, eggs, and fish and oysters from the sea. They bought local fruit and vegetables. But few of the troops were pleased to do military service in northern Britain. They wrote to their families in Gaul or Italy asking for warm socks and underwear.

△ **Remains of soldiers' tools used on the wall,** which included hammers, picks and trench-digging spades. Some of the troops who built Hadrian's Wall probably worked 20 years later on the smaller Antonine Wall in Scotland.

ROADS AND TRANSPORT

Travellers in Britain had plodded along trackways long before the Romans came. But the Romans needed paved, all-weather roads to carry heavy wagons and marching troops. They made highways all over their empire, and soon built a network of roads across Britain. Some modern British roads follow routes laid out by Roman engineers.

Of all Roman roads in Britain, the longest and straightest was the Fosse Way. It began at Exeter and crossed the country north-eastwards to the River Humber. The road was mainly a military route, dividing the Romanized south from the rest of Britain.

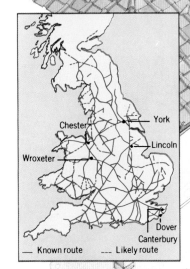

▷ **The road network in Roman Britain.** Roads from London included Watling Street, which ran north-west to Wroxeter and Chester. Other main roads led north to Lincoln and York, and south-east to Canterbury and Dover.

Known route ---- Likely route

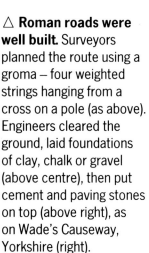

△ **Roman roads were well built.** Surveyors planned the route using a groma – four weighted strings hanging from a cross on a pole (as above). Engineers cleared the ground, laid foundations of clay, chalk or gravel (above centre), then put cement and paving stones on top (above right), as on Wade's Causeway, Yorkshire (right).

◁ **A typical Roman port or harbour.** Dover and London were important ports for cross-Channel trade. In London, quays and warehouses were built along the bank of the Thames. Flat-bottomed sailing barges carried building stone along the river. By the end of the Roman period, London was the busiest port in Britain.

▽ **A crowded street in a Midlands town in Roman Britain.**
A stonemason delivers building stone by cart. His tools are little different from hand-tools of today. The main street is crowded with women and children shopping, people on horseback, marching soldiers, coaches, wagons and litters carried on servants' shoulders.

Roads between the main settlements had forts along them for army use, but most routes were built for trade and to link towns. The Roman engineers began by building on ancient trackways, mostly on high, dry ground to avoid the forests and marshes. But to make more direct roads they had to use more difficult routes over various landscapes.

Roman roads were often, but not always, built straight. Because heavy wagons were hard to pull uphill, especially on a wet or icy road, mountain roads were made zigzag across the slope to make the climb less steep. On wet, boggy ground, engineers laid a base of timber and brushwood, or hammered in wooden piles to support the road.

Horses or oxen pulled vehicles that included four-wheeled wagons and coaches and smaller two-wheeled carts. Wealthy people also travelled in litters, carried by servants.

Ships, mostly from Gaul, docked at the ports of Richborough and Dover in Kent. To guide ships, the Romans built two lighthouses at Dover. Trade also passed through ports in the West Country, East Anglia and north-east England.

TRADE AND INDUSTRY

Roman Britain was rich. Farming flourished, and from mines came gold, silver, lead, iron ore and other minerals. Romans found the weather cold, but in many other ways Britain was profitable and pleasing. Under Roman rule, trade and industry developed. This in turn brought a rapid growth of towns.

▽ **Objects from a grave at St Albans,** from about AD 85. They show signs of wealth and a Romanized way of life.

Between three and four million people lived in Roman Britain, mostly in the countryside. Only about 250,000 people were town-dwellers.

The Romans had heard that Britain's farmland was fertile and that the land was rich in cattle, hides, grain, metals, slaves and hunting dogs. Under Roman rule, Britain's farmers produced even more food than before. But the Romans brought in other foods that they were used to. Wine came from Italy, Spain and Germany, and olive oil and fish sauce from Spain. They were stored in large jugs called amphorae.

All goods from abroad came by ship. Most of Britain's trade was across the Channel with Gaul. Roman soldiers wanted Roman goods, but when Britons joined the army, this demand fell.

▷ **Miners at work.** The hardest, most dangerous work was done by slaves or prisoners. Here, a man-powered treadmill works the machinery to pull out a sledge with baskets of iron ore. The southern Weald (Kent and Sussex) and the Forest of Dean in the west of England were the main iron-mining areas.

Money and goods

● Pieces of gold or coins were used to pay for trade within the Roman empire. The chief coins were the gold aureus, the silver denarius and the bronze sestertius.

● The smiths (see right) of Chichester formed one of Britain's first guilds, or trade associations.

● Leather (from animal skin) was much used. Most people wore leather sandals (see right and below). A legionary's shoes had hobnails hammered into the sole for extra wear.

● Glass was used to make beakers, bottles (see left) and windows.

△ **A blacksmith at work.** Smiths kept most of their skills secret so that no-one else could do their job.

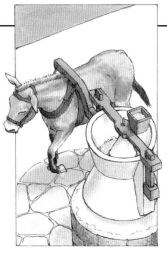

△ **A donkey-powered mill.** The Roman army ate vast amounts of grain, so farmers had to grow a lot of cereals, such as wheat.

△ **British potteries** often made cheap copies of the red-glazed beakers and pots that rich people imported from Gaul.

More industry, with new roads, public buildings and houses, made more work for engineers, stonemasons, tilers, carpenters and plumbers, and needed extra raw materials.

Gold came from the Dolaucothi mine in Wales. Lead and tin (which together make pewter, a metal used for pots and beakers) came from mines in the west and north. Builders burned limestone and chalk in kilns to make mortar and plaster, and smiths burned charcoal (charred wood) to smelt iron for tools, weapons and armour. Millers ground grain in water mills. Trees were cut down for wood to use as fuel.

British craftsmen made lots of cheap pottery and some glass, but most quality tableware and drinking glasses came from overseas. Britain was also famous for its textiles, especially woollen cloaks.

◁ **Water power was used in mining.** This waterwheel provides the power to drive a hammer. The hammer smashes the rocks to free the ore.

TOWNS OF ROMAN BRITAIN

The Romans liked town life. But most Roman towns were small. The poet Virgil wrote that "Rome stands out from all other cities as the cypress (tree) towers above lowly shrubs". In Britain, some towns were made for soldiers to retire to. Others grew through trade or were built on the old tribal strongholds.

Britons built the new towns themselves, but Roman army planners probably laid out the first ones at St Albans and Canterbury. Towns that were once tribal strongholds often used the local tribal name, such as Calleva Atrebatum (town in the wood of the Atrebates). Its name today is Silchester.

Roman towns were neat, with straight streets in a criss-cross pattern. At the main crossroads in the town centre was an open space called the forum. Shops and workplaces stood on three sides. On the fourth side was the basilica, or town hall and law courts.

▷ **Roman town life.** The forum was the town centre. There:
● news was given out, business deals made and goods traded
● stalls were set up on market days
● people went to worship at the temples.
   On public holidays, people went to the amphitheatre on the edge of town to watch gladiators (armed men) or animals fight.

△ **Shops opened on to the street.** Shopkeepers lived with their families in rooms at the back. To close the shops, they put up blinds or shutters.

▷ **The Newport Arch in Lincoln.** It is the only Roman arch in Britain still used by traffic today. Lincoln was developed by the Romans in AD 60.
● in about AD 200 a stone wall was built all the way round the town
● it had temples, a forum and a basilica
● there was a bath-house and several inns
● shops and houses were in all parts of the town.

Large towns had piped water, baths, drains and sewers. Some had amphitheatres. By AD 100, Cirencester, Exeter, Silchester, Winchester and St Albans all had fine public buildings of stone. Other buildings were wooden-framed.

Big towns were noisy, smelly and crowded, with streets full of people and carts. Large and small houses, shops, offices and workshops were all side by side, with few poor or 'slum' areas. Many towns grew outside army bases and some were set up for workers in pottery or mining industries.

Each town was governed by a council, which raised money from taxes on goods passing through the town, from rents, fines, and from the sale of water and minerals. London was Britain's biggest town by far, and by AD 100 it was capital of the province. Many of its people were merchants who, like businessmen and shopkeepers, might be freed slaves.

△ **Fruit and vegetables** came mainly from local farms. Cabbages, lettuces, radishes, turnips, parsnips, beans, peas, mushrooms and herbs were on sale.

△ **Excavation of the Roman forum and basilica at Caerwent in Wales.** Many Roman towns lie under our own city streets or close to modern roads, as here. Caerwent was a Roman town some 10 kilometres from the legionary fortress at Caerleon.

HOUSES AND HOMES

"Is there anything more hallowed (sacred) ... than the home of each citizen?", asked the Roman politician Cicero in about 50 BC. Romans in Italy built houses around small courtyards to keep out the sun. This was hardly necessary in Britain. But town houses and country villas were still built in Roman style.

▽ **These remains of a hypocaust** can be seen in the hot room of baths at Chedworth villa in Gloucestershire. Heat from a wood-burning furnace circulated under the floor.

Outside the towns, many Britons still lived in round huts. The first town houses in Britain had wooden frames and wattle and daub walls. Later houses were built of stone, at least on the ground floor. There were L-shaped houses, houses with two or more side extensions, as well as houses built around courtyards or gardens. The homes of rich people had bathrooms with water piped from the main supply.

Windows had shutters, bars, or glass that let in light but was not see-through. Extra light came from oil lamps or candles. Some houses had rooms with open hearths in the centre, as in the British huts. Others had rooms with fireplaces in walls. Wealthy owners could afford a hypocaust underfloor heating system, although many homes had this only for the dining room.

Most walls were plastered and painted inside and out. Rooms were decorated with scenes or patterns, or with painted columns and alcoves. Around AD 75, the Romans first used in Britain the tiny coloured tile patterning called mosaic, for floors. Floors were also made of larger tiles, wood, stone or marble. In poorer homes, the floor was hard-beaten earth with perhaps a rug or rush mat on top.

Most people had to fetch their water from public water tanks. Drains took waste water through sewers in the streets to the nearest river or stream. Water flowed continuously through the public lavatories, where Romans used wet sponges instead of lavatory paper.

▽ **Most people lived in smoky, draughty houses** similar to those of pre-Roman times. This farmer's homestead, with a thatched round house and a wooden barn, was common around AD 150.

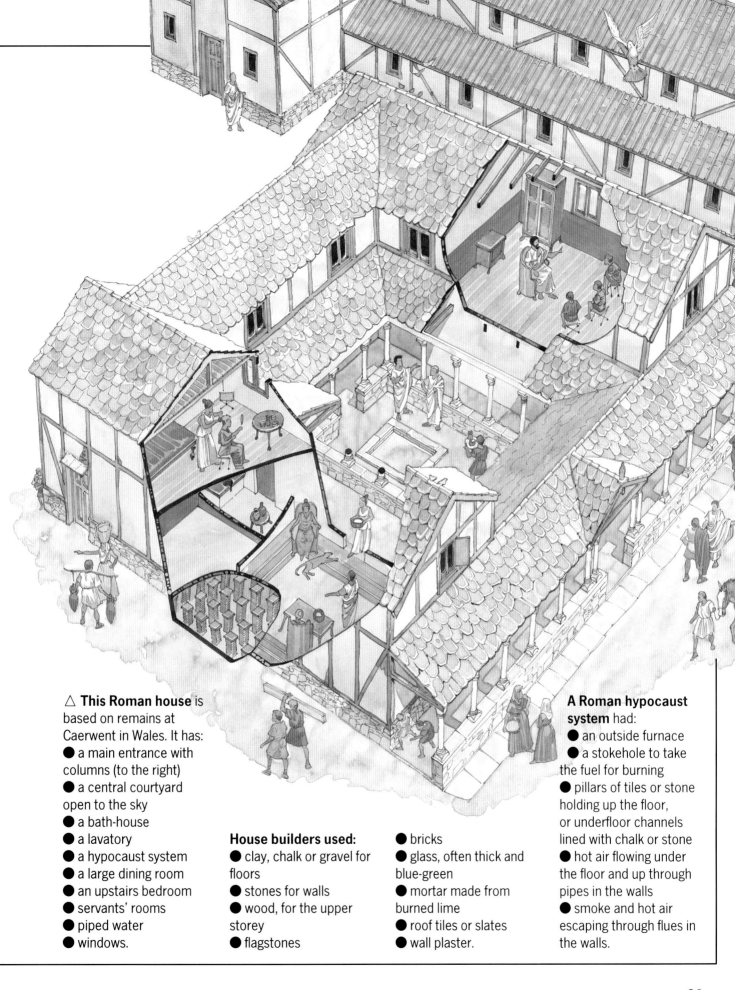

△ **This Roman house** is based on remains at Caerwent in Wales. It has:
● a main entrance with columns (to the right)
● a central courtyard open to the sky
● a bath-house
● a lavatory
● a hypocaust system
● a large dining room
● an upstairs bedroom
● servants' rooms
● piped water
● windows.

House builders used:
● clay, chalk or gravel for floors
● stones for walls
● wood, for the upper storey
● flagstones
● bricks
● glass, often thick and blue-green
● mortar made from burned lime
● roof tiles or slates
● wall plaster.

A Roman hypocaust system had:
● an outside furnace
● a stokehole to take the fuel for burning
● pillars of tiles or stone holding up the floor, or underfloor channels lined with chalk or stone
● hot air flowing under the floor and up through pipes in the walls
● smoke and hot air escaping through flues in the walls.

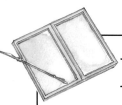

FAMILY LIFE

Family life was important to the Romans, as it was to the Celts. But the two peoples had different customs. Roman men were head of the family and masters of the house, yet women ran the household. Celtic women ruled tribes and led warriors. Roman ways changed some British lives greatly and others not at all.

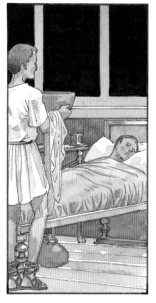

△ **Roman festivals** were linked to the seasons. This 'head of autumn' is on a mosaic from a villa in Cirencester, made in about AD 200.

△ **Household slaves** were treated better than those working in mines or workshops, and might buy freedom from their master with saved wages.

△ **Children of the household learnt** to read and write before the age of seven. Here a tutor is teaching older children at home.

△ **Many Britons learnt to speak and write Latin**, the Roman language used throughout the empire. Romans themselves often paid scribes, or trained writers, to keep lists, make records and write letters. They wrote on wax with a pointed iron pen called a stylus, as shown above, or with ink on wooden tablets or papyrus.

Letters were tied shut with string and sealed with wax or lead. They were delivered by hand.

Most people rose at dawn, and had a light breakfast or just a drink of water. In town, men often went to the local barber for a shave before starting work. Women (or slaves) cleaned the house, shopped, cooked, made clothes and taught the younger children. Rich families might have a slave or tutor to educate the older children. Romans on large farms also had slaves to help, or a manager to run the estate, and keep written records of goods bought and sold. On Celtic farms, the family shared the work, as they had always done. The day ended with the family's main meal, after which everyone went to bed.

△ Clothing
● Men and women wore tunics. On public occasions, Roman men wore the toga – a half-circle of cloth draped round the body.
● Outdoor wear included cloaks, hooded capes, and the wet-weather *byrrus Britannicus* – a long heavy wool or skin garment.
● Shoes had soles with nails to make them hard-wearing.
● People wore sandals in summer, as shown here.

△ **Roman homes had little furniture** apart from beds, couches and tables. Most was made from wood, and the rest from stone.

▷ **When people were ill, they sent for a doctor.** Roman doctors were highly trained, and treated wounds and infections, mended broken limbs and operated – without anaesthetics. Medicines were mainly made from herbs into pills, ointments and potions.

There were no weekends off work in Roman Britain, or annual holidays. But on religious festivals – every 10 days or so – people had free time. Some went to the amphitheatre or the races. Both Celts and Romans gambled, though it was against the law, and enjoyed hunting.

At home, people played board games and kept pets, such as dogs, cats and birds. Women wrote letters to family and friends and enjoyed hairdressing and fashion. Romans loved gardening, too, using plants in cooking and as medicines.

Parents often arranged their childrens' marriages, which took place at the bride's home. Girls could marry at 12, though most married later. Baby girls were named at eight days old and boys at nine days. During childhood they wore a good-luck charm round the neck.

Romans buried their dead in graves along the roads leading to town. Hired mourners and musicians joined funeral processions, which stopped in the forum to hear a speech honouring the dead person given by a relative or friend.

PALACES AND COUNTRY HOUSES

The great houses of Roman Britain were homes of chieftains, landowners and governors. Some, like the grand palace at Fishbourne, near Chichester in West Sussex, were official residences. Smaller country houses or villas were run as family homes.

In Roman Britain, a villa was a farm, with a farmhouse and outbuildings. A wealthy landowner might own several villas, and visit each during the year to check that the estate was being properly managed. Fishbourne may have been the home of Cogidubnus, a Celtic chief who became a Roman citizen.

Most British villas were modest homes, lived in by a family and its servants. Some small villas were rented from the owner by the farmer who worked the land.

Large or small, a villa was more 'Roman' than a native British house. From excavations of country villas, like the one at Chedworth near Cirencester in Gloucestershire, we know roughly what a Roman country home was like.

The house stood not far from a road. It was built of stone and wood, and the rooms were planned around a sunlit courtyard or garden. Gardeners planted hedges in patterns, with apple and pear trees, grape vines, rose bushes and herbs. Farmers grew carrots (used for medicine), peas, beans, onions and leeks. Wheat was the main cereal crop. Farm animals included cattle, sheep, pigs and geese. The villa provided bread, milk, meat and cheese for the local town and army garrison.

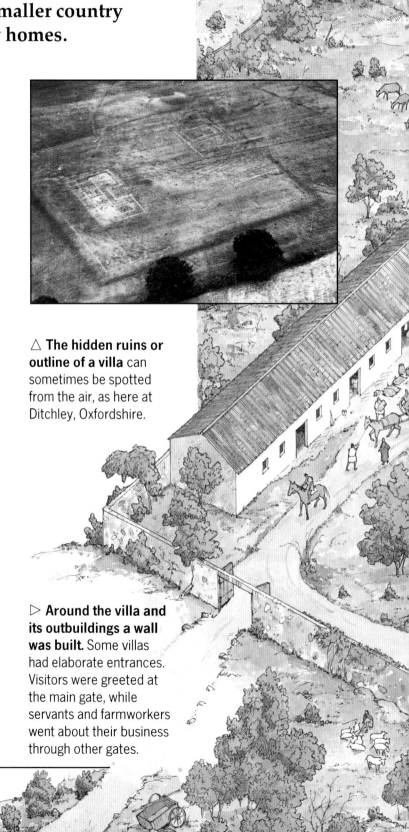

△ **The hidden ruins or outline of a villa** can sometimes be spotted from the air, as here at Ditchley, Oxfordshire.

▷ **Around the villa and its outbuildings a wall was built.** Some villas had elaborate entrances. Visitors were greeted at the main gate, while servants and farmworkers went about their business through other gates.

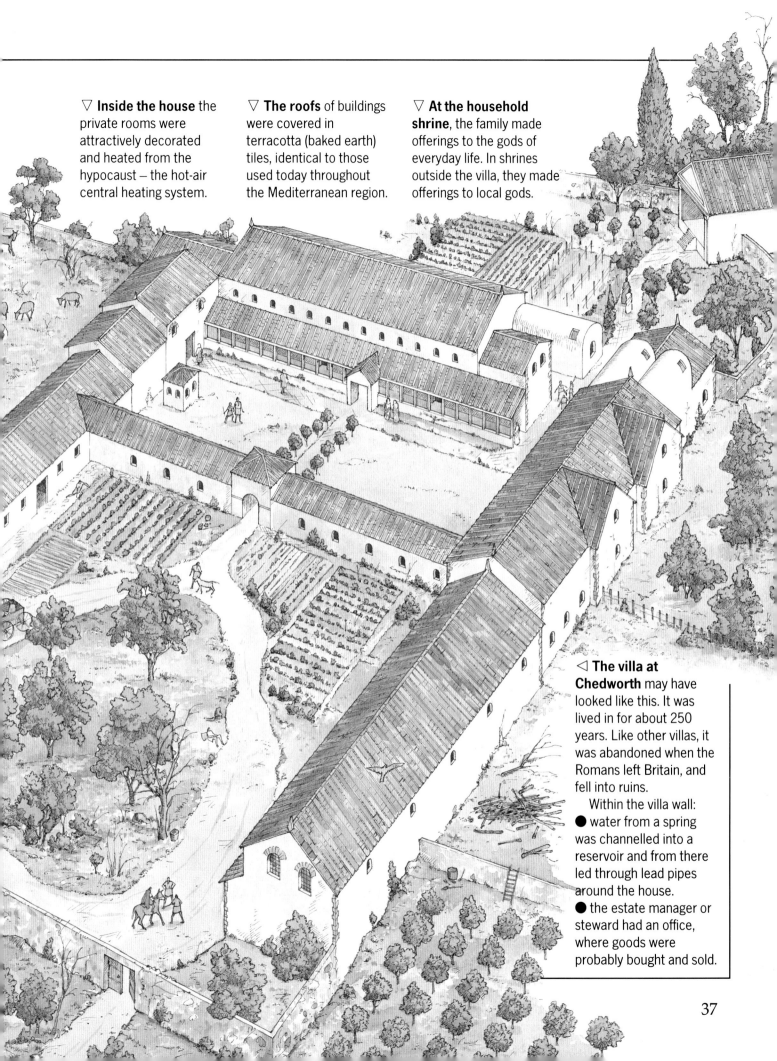

▽ **Inside the house** the private rooms were attractively decorated and heated from the hypocaust – the hot-air central heating system.

▽ **The roofs** of buildings were covered in terracotta (baked earth) tiles, identical to those used today throughout the Mediterranean region.

▽ **At the household shrine**, the family made offerings to the gods of everyday life. In shrines outside the villa, they made offerings to local gods.

◁ **The villa at Chedworth** may have looked like this. It was lived in for about 250 years. Like other villas, it was abandoned when the Romans left Britain, and fell into ruins.

Within the villa wall:
● water from a spring was channelled into a reservoir and from there led through lead pipes around the house.
● the estate manager or steward had an office, where goods were probably bought and sold.

COOKING AND EATING

Wealthy Romans enjoyed rich food and a varied diet. Ordinary families ate a lot of bread and porridge. Country people grew their own grain, fruit and vegetables, ground their own flour, and butchered their own meat. Town-dwellers had to buy their food from the local shops and markets.

Bakers' shops in Roman Britain sold white and brown bread. The loaves were round and either flat or cottage-loaf shaped. Remains of butchers' shops have also been found, and a meat market in Cirencester. The Roman seafood shop discovered at Wroxeter must have been one of many in Britain since shellfish and fish were popular and plentiful. Other shelled food included edible snails.

The Romans ate a lot of fish, but preferred fish sauces, which they used so much in cooking that they built large workshops to make vast quantities of it.

▷ **Reconstruction of a Roman kitchen.** Roman cooks used a wide range of herbs, spices and sauces. Food was boiled, fried, grilled and stewed. People enjoyed ready-cooked snacks of chops, sausages or fried chicken bought in the street. Among the meats Roman Britons ate were those of:
● oxen, sheep, goats, pigs, deer, boars, hares
● frogs
● ducks, geese, chickens
● swans, coots, thrushes.

▽ **In the kitchen**, some cooks were men, as here, but most were women. Food was cooked on stone hearths and in clay ovens. A few kitchens had piped hot water.

▷ **Meat joints, herbs and vegetables** hung from hooks in the roof. Other foods were stored in baskets, bowls or sacks. Liquids such as wine and sauces were kept in pottery jars. A large villa needed several kitchen staff, who were kept busy when their master was entertaining guests.

First course

Main course

Dessert

▷ **At Roman banquets,** the first course might be stuffed olives, roast dormice, oysters, snails or peacock eggs. The main course might be boar's head, chicken, lobsters or pigeons. For dessert, Romans ate fruit, honey cakes and stuffed dates.

▽ **Wealthy people ate lying on couches beside the table.** They:
● used cups, plates, knives and spoons
● ate most foods with their fingers, as here
● expected guests to bring their own cutlery and napkins.
 Breakfast was bread and cheese, or just water. Lunch was light: cold meat, vegetables, fruit. Dinner was the main family meal, eaten when the day's work was over.

Salt was used for adding flavour to food and for pickling. It came from the coast, or from salt springs inland, packed in barrels and jars. Olive oil for cooking and for lighting lamps was mostly imported from Spain.

Honey was used to sweeten foods and drinks. Country houses usually had their own beehives. Cheese was popular, but butter was rarely used. Romans thought milk fit only for children and invalids. Adults drank wine, which came from Spain, Italy, Africa, Greece and Gaul. The Britons still preferred beer and drank it in great amounts.

In traditional round houses, people cooked food over the fire. Most Roman houses and villas had a separate kitchen, and some families cooked in a separate building because of the smells and risk of fire. But much of their food was still cooked over a charcoal fire, in pots hung from tripods or standing on racks.

Country houses often had ovens for baking their own bread, but townspeople went to a bakery to buy theirs.

Few houses had fresh water pumped to the kitchen. Instead, slaves or the women of the house had to carry it in wooden buckets from the local well, fountain or public water trough.

GODS AND RELIGION

Religion played an important part in the everyday life of Roman Britain. Like the Celts, the Romans had many gods. Some were household gods, worshipped at home. Others were gods of the woods and fields. The year was marked by religious festivals at different seasons – such as seed-sowing time.

Most Roman families living in Britain kept a shrine in the house, a special place with an altar where they made gifts to various gods. The Lares were the spirits of the house itself. Vesta was the goddess of the hearth-fire, the Penates were spirits of the storeroom. Janus (a two-faced god) was the guardian spirit of the door. The head of the family would lead the religious ceremonies. Sometimes an animal was killed as a sacrifice to bring peace and prosperity to family, house and town.

The Romans, like the Celts, were very superstitious. They believed that omens such as a strange-shaped cloud, a storm, or a flight of birds could tell the future. Soothsayers or fortune-tellers also looked at the insides of dead animals, to discover good or bad news.

The Romans borrowed religious beliefs and customs from people all over their empire. For a time the emperors made themselves gods. So British gods were adopted quite happily by the Romans. Soldiers brought their own gods; some, like Isis and Mithras, came from the East. There was a temple to Mithras on Hadrian's Wall and an underground temple to Mithras has been discovered in London.

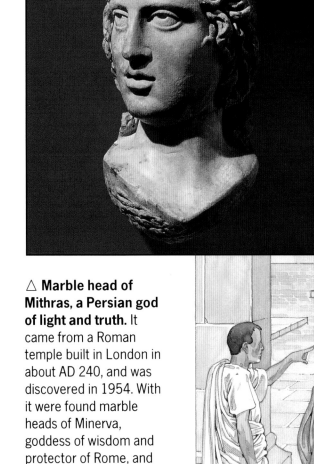

△ **Marble head of Mithras, a Persian god of light and truth.** It came from a Roman temple built in London in about AD 240, and was discovered in 1954. With it were found marble heads of Minerva, goddess of wisdom and protector of Rome, and Serapis, Egyptian god of the underworld. Soldiers liked Mithras's qualities of courage and loyalty.

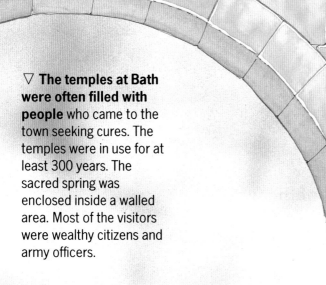

▽ **The temples at Bath were often filled with people** who came to the town seeking cures. The temples were in use for at least 300 years. The sacred spring was enclosed inside a walled area. Most of the visitors were wealthy citizens and army officers.

▽ **Tall stone columns, carved friezes and statues** made the Bath temples among the most elegant in Roman Britain. This shrine belonged to the goddess Sul Minerva.

△ **Romans believed that household gods** watched over every family. This is a small private altar in a house. Usually the father of the family acted as the priest.

△ **Each region of Britain had local gods.** People set up shrines to them, like this one in honour of a god of the Brigantes of northern Britain.

▷ **This mosaic floor picture from a villa in Dorset** is possibly an early British portrait of Jesus Christ. Christianity became the religion of the Roman empire during the reign of the emperor Constantine the Great (AD 306-337). Some families in Britain had Christian chapels in their homes.

The town of Bath, with its hot springs, had fine temples in the Roman style. People went to the temples to worship a healing goddess called Sul Minerva to seek cures. They also visited another temple at Lydney in Gloucestershire, which was sacred to a British healing god named Nodens. Roman and British religions became thoroughly mixed. By about AD 300 some people in Roman Britain were Christians. By AD 400, Christianity was the main religion.

ROMAN BRITAIN ENDS

Britain prospered in the early 4th century, when many villas were enlarged. But 100 years later, the Roman army had gone. It was needed elsewhere in the empire – even in Rome itself – to fight off hostile tribes. These invaders were the 'barbarians', among them the Huns, Goths, Vandals, Franks and Saxons.

The Roman empire was breaking up. Rome was ruled by weak emperors, afraid of being overthrown by barbarians or by their own discontented generals. Rome could no longer govern or defend distant provinces. Britain was at the edge of the crumbling empire. It was open both to foreign invaders and to local governors with ambitions to seize power.

The army tried to defend Britain. From about AD 280, forts were built on the south and east coasts to face attacks from Saxon pirates. Ships of the British fleet also guarded the Channel and North Sea against pirate raids. Around 286 the commander of the fleet, Carausius, seized Britain and declared himself emperor.

▽ **Saxons attack a Roman town in southern England,** burning public buildings and looting shops. Barbarians who came to southern and eastern Britain from Denmark and Germany were:
● Saxons
● Jutes
● Angles.
The Roman empire was overrun by:
● Vandals from Germany
● Visigoths from southern Europe
● Franks and Burgundians from France and Germany
● Ostrogoths.

△ **An aerial view of the Roman walls (and medieval buildings) of Porchester**, at Portsmouth. This was a fort of the Saxon Shore, built to fight off invaders.

△ **Saxon copy of a Roman map** showing forts built to keep out Saxon raiders. Such forts were built over Britain and on the north-east coast of Gaul.

△ **A coin of Magnus Maximus**, dated from about 380. Generals who seized power, like Carausius and Maximus, made their own coins to pay their soldiers.

As the Roman army departed (shown right), the Britons had to defend themselves. In such troubled times, people sometimes buried their valuables. A famous hoard since found is the Mildenhall Treasure, from Suffolk.

Roman troops landed to reclaim Britain in 296. Defences were strengthened and the island again prospered. But in 367, three tribes – the Picts, Scots and Allocotti – all invaded at once. The army lost control. Soldiers deserted and looters roamed the country. Rome sent a general called Theodosius to restore order.

In 383 another British commander, Magnus Maximus, made himself emperor and took most of the army from Britain. In 398 barbarian tribes again invaded. Roman troops under orders from a leader called Stilicho came to fight them.

In 406 Roman troops in Britain again elected their own emperor. But so many German invaders had crossed the River Rhine into Gaul that Britain was now cut off from Rome. The last Roman soldiers left in Britain were sent to fight in Gaul.

Britons now faced, alone, the Saxons from the sea. In 410 the emperor Honorius wrote a letter to the British cities telling them to look after their own defence. Roman Britain was at an end.

FAMOUS PEOPLE OF ROMAN TIMES

Gnaeus Julius Agricola (37-93) was one of Rome's best generals. As governor of Britain he conquered the northern part of the country, as far as Scotland (see pages 18 and 19).

Augustus Caesar (63 BC – AD 14), also known as Octavianus, was the first Roman emperor, from 27 BC to AD 14.

Aulus Plautius (first century AD) was the Roman general who commanded the invasion in AD 43. He became first Roman governor of Britain.

Boudicca (died in AD 60) was the British queen of the Iceni. She led a revolt against the Romans but was defeated by Suetonius Paulinus (see page 17).

Queen Boudicca

Caratacus (first century AD) was the British chief of the Catuvellauni, son of Cunobelinus. He fought the Romans but was finally captured and sent with his family to Rome (see pages 14, 15, 16).

Marcus Aurelius Carausius (died 293) was a Roman soldier who led the Classis Britannicus, or British fleet, against the Franks and

Saxons (see page 42). He made himself emperor and ruled Britain from 286 until he was murdered by a rival.

Cartimandua (first century AD) was queen of the Brigantes, and an ally of Rome (see page 16). Her ex-husband Venutius fought the Romans.

Cassivellaunus (first century BC) was ruler of the Catuvellauni of Hertfordshire and led a combined British force against the invasion of Julius Caesar (see page 13).

Claudius (10 BC-AD 54) was Roman emperor from AD 41 to 54. He visited Britain in triumph after the invasion of AD 43 (see page 15).

Cogidubnus (died AD 75) was prince of the Atrebates, a tribe of southern Britain (see pages 30, 36). The Romans allowed him to stay as a local ruler, and he may have lived in the great house found at Fishbourne in West Sussex.

Constantine the Great (275-337) was the first Roman emperor to become a Christian. He was declared emperor while with the Roman army at York.

Emperor Constantine

Cunobelinus was the most powerful British king before the Roman invasion (see page 14). His capital was Colchester. His son Caratacus fought the Romans.

Julius Frontinus (first century AD) was Roman governor of Britain from about 73 to 78. He began the Roman conquest of Wales (see page 18).

Gaius Julius Caesar (100-44 BC) was probably the most famous Roman of all. A general and statesman, he conquered Gaul and invaded Britain twice (see pages 12, 13). Emperor Augustus was his adopted son.

Hadrian (AD 76-138) was Roman emperor from 117 to 138. He ordered the building of the wall in north Britain bearing his name (see pages 24, 25).

Magnus Maximus (died AD 388) was a Roman soldier who fought the Picts and Scots (see page 43). His troops proclaimed him emperor and he ruled the west of the empire until he was captured and executed by the Eastern emperor Theodosius.

Magnus Maximus

Prasutagus (first century AD) was chief of the Iceni (see page 17). His wife, Boudicca, was not allowed by the Romans to take over leadership of the tribe when he died.

Flavius Stilicho (AD 365-408) was a skilful Roman general in the West who fought the barbarians but was later accused of treason and executed. He may have come to Britain with troops in 398 (see page 43).

Flavius Stilicho

Suetonius Paulinus (first century AD) was Roman governor of Britain in AD 58-61. He captured the Druid stronghold of Anglesey and then defeated Boudicca's army (see pages 16, 17).

Tacitus (AD 56-120) was a Roman historian. He wrote histories of the Roman empire, descriptions of German tribes and a life history of General Agricola. His account of the conquest of Britain is the most detailed we have.

Vespasian (AD 9-79) was Roman emperor from 68 to 79. He fought in Britain as a legionary commander during the invasion of AD 43 (see page 14).

BRITISH TRIBES AND ROMAN EMPERORS

The map below shows the territories of the major tribes of Britain at the time of Claudius's conquest in AD 43. The boundaries of these territories were constantly changing as tribes fought each other for land, food and wood.

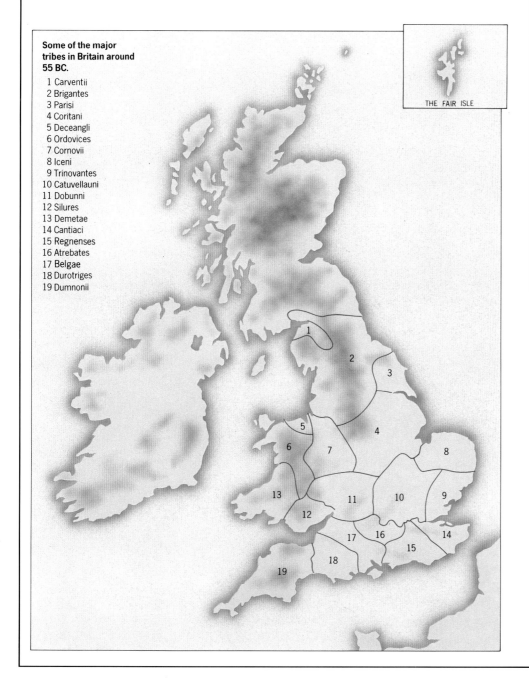

Some of the major tribes in Britain around 55 BC.

1 Carventii
2 Brigantes
3 Parisi
4 Coritani
5 Deceangli
6 Ordovices
7 Cornovii
8 Iceni
9 Trinovantes
10 Catuvellauni
11 Dobunni
12 Silures
13 Demetae
14 Cantiaci
15 Regnenses
16 Atrebates
17 Belgae
18 Durotriges
19 Dumnonii

THE FAIR ISLE

GLOSSARY

alliance an agreement, between allies or friendly groups, to work or fight together.

amphitheatre bowl-shaped arena where spectators watched games and gladiator fights.

amphora tall jar for storing liquids such as olive oil.

artillery weapons used to hurl missiles, such as catapults and giant crossbows.

banquet a grand meal, with lots of food.

barbarian the Romans thought anyone who did not speak Latin was a barbarian, an uncivilized person.

barrow mound of earth over the burial place of a Celt.

basilica building in a Roman town, used for public ceremonies.

cavalry soldiers on horseback.

centurion Roman officer in command of 80 to 100 soldiers.

charcoal partly burnt wood, used in furnaces, especially for iron-making.

citizen a person (usually a man) who was allowed to vote in elections for governors and other leaders.

craftsmen people who earned their living by a skill or special trade, such as blacksmiths, potters, shoemakers.

emperor supreme ruler of Rome; the first emperor was Augustus.

forum market place or public meeting area in a town, with public buildings around it.

frontier boundary between one territory and another.

gladiators trained fighters who fought in the arena. Some slaves were made gladiators.

hypocaust central heating system in houses, using underfloor hot air.

iron ore iron in its natural state, mixed up with other substances in rock.

Latin language of the Romans.

legion main unit of the Roman army, with 5,000 to 6,000 soldiers.

merchants people who made their living by buying and selling things, either in their own country or abroad.

mosaic floor or wall made up of small cubes of coloured stone, glass or other hard substance arranged to make pictures or patterns.

revolt uprising against the people running the country, to try to replace them.

rite religious ceremony or prayer to a god.

smelt to separate pure iron from iron ore by heating it in a furnace.

standard ceremonial pole carried into battle by the legion, a rallying point for the troops.

taxes money collected by the government from the people to pay for new roads, buildings or to equip the army.

toga Roman citizen's outer clothing, made from a large piece of cloth draped around the body.

villa usually a farm with a house and outbuildings, but also a large country house.

PLACES TO VISIT

In town museums all over Britain there are examples of Roman or pre-Roman pottery and coins. These are some of the best places to visit.

Antonine Wall (Scotland), best-preserved remains at Watling Lodge and Rough Castle.

Avebury (Wiltshire) Large pre-Roman henge monument (standing stones, chalk bank and ditch), with museum.

Bath (Avon) Roman baths and other buildings, museum.

Bignor (Sussex) Parts of villa can be seen.

Butser (Hampshire) Reconstructed Iron Age farm.

Caerleon (Wales) Legionary fortress, barracks, amphitheatre and museum.

Caerwent (Wales) Walls, gates and defences can still be seen.

Canterbury (Kent) Remains of Roman town house, with mosaic floors and hypocaust.

Chedworth (Gloucestershire) Museum and excavated remains of villa.

Chester (Cheshire) Museum and remains of Roman defences and amphitheatre (perhaps the biggest in Britain).

Chichester (Sussex) City and Guildhall museums have Roman-British pottery and coins.

Cirencester (Gloucestershire) Museum, sections of town wall, remains of amphitheatre.

Colchester (Essex) Museum with models illustrating Roman town.

Dorchester (Dorset) Museum, amphitheatre.

Dover (Kent) Remains of lighthouse on clifftop inside Dover Castle.

Fishbourne (West Sussex) Remains of so-called palace of Cogidubnus.

Hadrian's Wall (Cumbria, Tyne and Wear) Sections of wall and forts such as Housesteads, Vindolanda, Carrawburgh.

Hod Hill (Dorset) Iron Age hill-fort and small Roman fort.

Lincoln (Lincolnshire) Museum, parts of gates and town walls; also sections of Roman road north and south.

Little Woodbury (Wiltshire) Reconstruction of Iron Age village.

London British Museum and Museum of London; remains of Roman city wall, plan of Temple of Mithras (11 Queen Victoria Street).

Lullingstone (Kent) Museum, parts of Roman villa.

Maiden Castle (Dorset) Enormous hill-fort and mounds to walk over.

Richborough (Kent) Remains of shore defences, monument and Saxon Shore fort.

Silbury Hill (Wiltshire) Great mound built by stone-using people about 2150 BC.

Silchester (Hampshire) Museum and amphitheatre; most of the Roman town is now beneath farmland.

St Albans (Hertfordshire) Verulamium Museum, walls, theatre, remains of Celtic settlement.

Stonehenge (Wiltshire) Finest religious site of the bronze-using people in Europe, with standing stones set up between about 2150 BC and 1250 BC.

York (North Yorkshire) Museum and remains of legionary fortress, partly under the medieval cathedral or Minster.

INDEX

48